FOOTBALL HALL OF **FAMERS**

DEACON JONES

Karen Donnelly

the rosen publishing group's
rosen
central

Published in 2003 by The Rosen Publishing Group, Inc.
29 East 21st Street, New York, NY 10010

Copyright © 2003 by The Rosen Publishing Group, Inc.

First Edition

Library of Congress Cataloging-in-Publication Data

Donnelly, Karen J.
Deacon Jones / Karen Donnelly.— 1st ed.
    p. cm. — (Football Hall of Famers)
Summary: Profiles the Los Angeles Rams' football player
whose techniques changed the way coaches and fans
thought about defense and caused him to be named
"Defensive End of the Century" by Sports Illustrated.
Includes bibliographical references and index.
ISBN 0-8239-3606-6 (lib. bdg.)
1. Jones, Deacon, 1938-—Juvenile literature. 2. Football
players—United States—Biography—Juvenile literature.
[1. Jones, Deacon, 1938- 2. Football players. 3. African
Americans—Biography.]
I.Title. II. Series.
GV939.J63 D66 2003
796.332'092—dc21

                                        2002000280

Manufactured in the United States of America

Contents

Known as the Secretary of Defense, Deacon Jones was voted Most Valuable Defensive Player twice, in 1967 and 1968. Jones left a permanent stamp on football with his invention of the "sack." He was named to the NFL's all-time team put together in 1994 to commemorate the league's seventy-fifth anniversary.

Introduction

In the early days of football, the defensive line was made of slow, heavy giants who blocked the oncoming offense like a rock wall. Nobody expected a defensive lineman to attack, run, or chase the opponent's quarterback in his own backyard.

When Deacon Jones joined the defensive line of the Los Angeles Rams in 1961, he changed those expectations. Plain and simple: Jones was fast. He charged over the line of scrimmage, slapping the helmet of any offensive lineman who had the nerve to try to block him. He dropped quarterbacks in the backfield so often that opposing coaches sent two or three players after him. Deacon Jones, however, was simply unstoppable.

Deacon Jones changed the way coaches and fans thought about defense, earning the nickname "the Secretary of Defense." With Merlin Olsen, Lamar Lundy, and Roosevelt "Rosey" Grier, he rounded out the Rams' defense. Together, they were so effective at rushing the passer that they became known as "the Fearsome Foursome."

But Jones's talents alone were not enough to make success come easily in his football career. During the 1950s and 1960s, the United States was struggling through the beginnings of the Civil Rights movement. Racial prejudice was widespread. Even on the football field, where players should be judged by their ability, African American players had to fight discrimination. Any complaints caused a player to be labeled a troublemaker. Often the outspoken player was traded off his team.

While Jones was not afraid to speak out against racial prejudice, he made most of his points on the football field. He led the new breed of defensive linemen, making the defense exciting to watch. He became the National

Dave "Deacon" Jones's style of defense consisted of first clearing the offensive player he was assigned to with a "head-slap" (now banned) and then taking on the quarterback head on. "I left blood out there," he recalled in an Associated Press interview. "I put the fear of God in the whole league."

Football League's (NFL) Most Valuable Defensive Player in 1967 and 1968. Unofficially, he is credited with 180.5 sacks over his career (the NFL did not recognize the sack as an official statistic until 1982). He played in eight Pro Bowls and was named to the NFL's seventy-fifth anniversary team. Deacon Jones was inducted into the NFL Hall of Fame in 1980, the first year he became eligible.

Early Life

Before he was known to the football world as "Deacon," David Jones was known to his seven brothers and sisters as "Davey." Born in 1938 to Mattie and Ishmeal Jones, he grew up in Eatonville, Florida, at a time when southern society was segregated, separating African Americans from whites.

Jones's family was lucky because Ishmeal had a job. Even so, by the time Davey was twelve, he was already working to help support his family. He took on any job he could find. When watermelons were ready to be picked in the fields outside Eatonville, he spent hours pitching melons from the field to a catcher in the back of a truck. It was backbreaking work, but without his help, Jones's family would not have been able to make ends meet.

The Segregated South

In 1952, life in the South was very different for African Americans than it was for whites. Signs reading "whites only" hung over water fountains and on the doors of restrooms. Jones and his family had to ride in the back of a bus because the front seats were reserved for whites. If the back rows of seats were filled, Jones had to stand, even if the front seats were empty. Restaurants had whites-only seating areas, often requiring that African Americans walk around to a window in the back to pick up their food.

The U.S. Supreme Court had ruled that "separate but equal" was allowed, so white children did not go to school with African American children. Unfortunately, no one checked to be sure that the separate schools were really equal. African American children went to rundown schools with few books. White children often enjoyed bright, airy, well-equipped classrooms.

African American families lived together in towns like Eatonville, outside the all-white towns they were allowed to enter only for work.

THIS DOOR
WHITE ONLY
COLORED IN REAR

Racial segregation was a fact of life in the South until the late 1960s. African Americans were confronted by signs like this at public places such as parks, bus depots, and eateries. As a child, Deacon had to drink from blacks-only water fountains, use blacks-only restrooms, and sit in blacks-only sections of restaurants.

Walking alone in an all-white town could be dangerous for an African American. Jones knew that white strangers in Eatonville probably also meant trouble.

One Sunday, Jones, his family, and friends gathered outside their church following the morning service. Jones saw a car racing down the dirt road so fast it stirred up a cloud of dust. As the car got closer, Jones could tell that it was a shiny, yellow convertible, an unusual sight in Eatonville, filled with white high school kids. As the car passed the church, one of the passengers stood up in the backseat and threw a watermelon toward the churchgoers. Jones yelled, warning everyone to look out. Most people were able to move out of the way. However, not everyone was fast enough. The melon crashed down on an old woman, knocking her to the ground, where her head smacked against a stone. Blood streamed from her nose and ears.

Today the police would be expected to track down and arrest the driver of the yellow convertible and his friends. But in 1952, the police would not necessarily have been concerned by what they would consider an unfortunate accident. The white teenagers, the police would have believed, were only playing a joke and had not intended to hit anyone with the watermelon.

Fighting for Equal Rights

Most adults in Eatonville believed that they were powerless to fight segregation. Soon, however, individual citizens began to stand up against racial injustice. In 1955, in Montgomery, Alabama, Rosa Parks refused to give up her bus seat to a white man. Her single action led to a bus boycott, one of the first acts of civil disobedience that would be central to the Civil Rights movement. Soon, more and more African Americans began ignoring the laws that enforced racial discrimination. In 1960, in Greensboro, North Carolina, four African American students sat at a white lunch counter and refused to leave until they were served.

Change came slowly. In Eatonville, Davey Jones became more and more angry at the unfair treatment that he and his friends received. He

Rosa Parks is fingerprinted by deputy sheriff D.H. Lackey in Montgomery, Alabama, on February 22, 1956 after her arrest for refusing to give her bus seat to a white passenger. This simple act violating segregation laws led to a boycott of buses by blacks, adding momentum to the civil rights movement.

never forgot the old woman who had been hit with the watermelon. She had never recovered and had died a few months after the "accident." Jones could not understand why white people wanted to treat African Americans so unfairly. Most of all, he could not understand why African Americans stood for it.

A few years later, Jones and some of his high school friends got the chance to watch Jackie Robinson play baseball for the Brooklyn

Dodgers. Before Robinson began playing first base for the Dodgers in 1947, African Americans had been forced to play only in the Negro baseball leagues. When Robinson crossed the line into major league baseball he opened a door for other African American athletes. The path to integration, however, would not be easy.

Davey Jones and his friends saw Jackie Robinson's struggle first hand. At one point, after hitting the ball into right field, Robinson slid into second base. The second baseman stepped down hard on Robinson's hand, grinding his cleats into Robinson's flesh. Seemingly unfazed, Robinson stood up. Instead of fighting with the second baseman, Robinson took off on the next pitch and stole third base.

After the game, Jones and his friends stood in line to get Jackie Robinson's autograph. This close to his hero, Jones began to think about his own future. He did not want to spend the rest of his life pitching watermelons. More than anything, he wanted to get out of Eatonville. He had to find a way.

Jackie Robinson

Jack Roosevelt Robinson, born on January 31, 1919, was the youngest son of a Georgia sharecropper. During his college career at UCLA, Robinson excelled at basketball, football, and track and field in addition to baseball. After serving time in the army, Robinson joined the Negro leagues' Kansas City Monarchs.

Branch Rickey, general manager of the Brooklyn Dodgers, scouted the Negro leagues for a player he thought could break the barrier that kept African American players from competing with white players. In 1946, Rickey chose Robinson, signing him to play for the Dodgers' farm team, the Montreal Royals. On April 15, 1947, Robinson became the first African American to play major league baseball in the twentieth century.

In his first season, Robinson held the National League record for stolen bases and was second in runs scored. He was named Rookie of the Year and led the Dodgers to a pennant victory. Throughout his ten-year career, Robinson played in six World Series, six all-star games, and in 1949 was named the National League's Most Valuable Player. His lifetime batting average was .317.

Jackie Robinson became the first African American to play in major league baseball in the twentieth century when he joined the Brooklyn Dodgers in 1947. The end of the color barrier, however, did not mean racism was over. African American athletes in all sports still faced many hurdles.

The Road Out of Eatonville

Jones knew that his best chance for a ticket out of Eatonville would be through professional sports. He spent his high school years at Hungerford High. The Hungerford High Bobcats football team were a powerhouse in their league. In 1956, Jones's senior year, he played as a tackle on both the offense and defense, helping to earn his team another winning season. With his outstanding record, he had expected to hear from college scouts. Without an athletic scholarship, he would never get to college. Jones was sure that without college no professional team would ever sign him.

Unfortunately, while Jones's talent had impressed his coach, Ed Clark, his outspoken attitude seemed to work against him. Jones was not afraid to tell the coach when he thought the wrong play had been called. Like most coaches, Clark did not like to hear criticism from his young players. He believed his team should carry out the plays that he called and learn from them. Jones realized that Clark probably had told the college scouts he was a troublemaker. Although there were still a few months before graduation, Jones knew that without Clark's recommendation, his chances of being offered a football scholarship were slim.

Jones's worries became reality after graduation. He had received his diploma but no scholarship offers. Jones and his friends decided to strike out on their own. They would travel to New York, work in the fields upstate and make enough money to move to New York City. As they talked about their dreams, they became more and more convinced that they would make it to the big city and get high-paying jobs.

Jones and his friends arranged to share a ride to New York. Right away, their dreams began to fizzle away. The driver demanded payment of $25 before he would leave. That was almost all the money Jones had brought. The rest of the money was gone by the time they got to New York. They were able to get jobs

The APFA

On September 17, 1920, in Canton, Ohio, the American Professional Football Association, the forerunner of the modern NFL, was born. Ten teams agreed on rules and regulations and named Jim Thorpe, the most famous football player of that era, to be president. On September 26, 1920, the Rock Island (Illinois) Independents rolled over the St. Paul (Minnesota) Ideals 48–0 in the first game of the APFA. In October, the Muncie (Indiana) Flyers ran out of money and disbanded. The APFA continued its season with the remaining teams.

Jim Thorpe (1887–1953) is considered by many as the greatest athlete of the twentieth century. He won the gold in the decathlon and pentathlon events in the 1912 Olympics and played major league baseball for six years before turning to his favorite sport, football. As halfback, he led the Canton Bulldogs to unofficial championships in 1916, 1917, and 1919. A Native American with some French and Irish blood, Thorpe also had an Indian name that meant "Bright Path." Thorpe was inducted into the Football Hall of Fame in its first year of opening, 1963, and also has a town named after him in northern Pennsylvania.

picking beans right away. Unfortunately, the pay was no better than the wages they had earned in Florida. Now they had to pay for their own food and other expenses, in addition. They ended up with far less money than they would have made if they had stayed home. The money they were able to save was not enough to get them to New York City. It was not even enough to get them home.

Jones decided to call his parents. He hoped they would send him $200, enough money to get to the city. Although his mother agreed to send the money, she quickly changed her mind. She believed in her son and knew he could get to college. To do that however, he would need to come home to Eatonville.

Jones and his friends never made it to New York City, but they did make it back to Eatonville. Jones realized that picking vegetables would never lead to a better life. He decided that with or without a scholarship, he would go to college.

From College
to the Pros

few years earlier, Deacon Jones's dream of playing professional football would have been impossible. From 1904 through 1933, only thirty African Americans had played in the pros. After that, no African Americans played in the National Football League until the color barrier was finally broken in 1946 when the Los Angeles Rams signed Kenny Washington and Woody Strode. That same year Bill Willis and Marion Motley joined the Cleveland Browns. Gradually during the 1950s and 1960s, other NFL teams signed a few African American players. While this was progress, the teams were far from integrated. Most teams had only two, three, or four African American players—never more than six. African

American players were not allowed to play the "glamour" positions, such as quarterback. They were always stuck on the line, where they could only block and tackle.

These drawbacks did not stop Davey Jones. He wanted to play in the NFL and he would do whatever it took to get himself there. The first step was to get on a college team. Despite his outstanding high school play, this task would not be an easy one. Unfortunately for Jones, his performance in the classroom had not kept up with his football success.

Frederick Douglass "Fritz" Pollard

Frederick Douglass "Fritz" Pollard, the sixth African American player in professional football, was the first African American head coach. In 1920 Pollard coached the Akron (Ohio) Pros to an 8–3 record. Pollard had played in the Pros backfield beginning in 1919. He continued his career on the playing field until 1926.

Getting to College

Jones first looked to his older brother, Judson, to help him. Judson Jones had been a Black All-American in 1952 and 1953 at Xavier College in New Orleans. Unfortunately, despite his own success, Judson Jones was not able to convince Xavier to overlook his brother's poor grades and accept him based only on his athletic ability.

Davey Jones's luck would soon change, however. Jones's friend, Roosevelt Steays, had played for two years at South Carolina State. Although Steays had been a year ahead of Jones at Hungerford High, they had played several seasons together. Steays knew how big and quick Jones was. Steays convinced his coach at South Carolina that they needed Jones to strengthen their defensive line.

Jones was going to college after all. Although South Carolina State, a small college in Orangeburg, was not a school that would attract professional scouts, they played larger schools like Florida A & M.

Deacon Jones accepts congratulations from South Carolina State University's head football coach Willie Jeffries during a ceremony held to retire the former college and NFL football star's college jersey in 1998.

In September 1957, Davey Jones's dream had turned from impossible to possible.

Once on the field, Jones devoted himself entirely to becoming the best football player he could be. College football was harder than high school ball, so Jones concentrated all his efforts on improving his skills as a tackle.

Once again, that meant sacrificing his studying. For Jones, college was all about football, not grades. Football had gotten him out of Eatonville and football would be his ticket to a better future.

Jones had made the first step toward that future by making it to a college team. Now he needed to get noticed. Finally, he got his opportunity. South Carolina State would take on Florida A & M. Jones's coach let him know that a pro scout would be at the game to watch one of the Florida players. Jones knew this was his big chance, and he did not waste it. He was all over the field, even intercepting a pass. South Carolina State lost the game, but Jones had made a big impression on Eddie Kotal, scout for the Los Angeles Rams.

Rams History

The Cleveland Rams were founded in 1937 by Homer Marshman, an attorney. Dan Reeves bought the team in 1941. In 1946, Reeves requested permission to move his team to Los Angeles. Other owners objected. They did not want to pay the money to travel to the West Coast to play. Reeves agreed to pay each team $5,000 to cover extra travel expenses when they played the Rams in Los Angeles. The National Football League approved the deal. The Rams became the first professional team to move to California, playing their first season in Los Angeles in 1947.

In 1995, the Rams became the first NFL team to move east. They now make their home in St. Louis, Missouri.

Marching for Civil Rights

While Jones would have preferred to concentrate every waking moment on football, the world would not let him. The civil rights movement was heating up in 1958, and college campuses were the center of activity. The questions Jones had asked all his life—why he, his family, and his friends were forced to the back of the bus and out of restaurants—were now being asked by greater numbers of people. African Americans were taking a stand against the injustices that had kept them second-class citizens; they were demanding to be treated as equals. They wanted the old rules changed, and they were willing to fight to make that happen.

College students at South Carolina State began organizing sit-ins, a form of non-violent protest. One of their favorite targets was the local bus station, which enforced many of the whites-only rules. Students sat outside the station with signs, protesting the restrictions. They also marched peacefully through downtown Orangeburg.

One Sunday, Jones and some of his teammates joined the marchers. Jones was amazed to find crowds of white people lining the streets, shouting, waving their fists, and throwing rocks and bottles. The police arrived, but not to protect the marchers. Instead, the police used dogs to chase the marchers. They began running in all directions. Jones ran into an

alley where men sprayed a fire hose on him. The force of the water slammed him against the fence.

Jones and his friends were arrested and spent the night in a barbed-wire pen. This would be Jones's last civil rights protest. He believed in the fight against injustice. However, he knew that nonviolent protesting was not something he could continue. He was afraid his anger would lead him to violence. To avoid this danger, Jones decided to stay away from civil rights demonstrations.

Ironically, Jones's decision came too late. As a result of the march that had led to Jones's arrest, local authorities in Orangeburg demanded that the president of South Carolina State do something to stop the protests. Under pressure, the president took away the football scholarships of those players who had participated in the march. Without the scholarship, Deacon Jones would have to leave the school.

Moving to Mississippi

Dejected and filled with rage against injustice, Jones wondered what to do. How could he get to the pros if he was not in college? It was his good fortune to find a new opportunity right away. The head coach at Mississippi Vocational College in Greenwood offered Jones and the other ousted South Carolina State players a chance to play. Mississippi Vocational required that its students be Mississippi residents, so Jones and his friends would need to use false names and pretend to be from Mississippi. This habit of hiding players was common at many schools. Jones decided he would take the risk in order to play.

Thanks to Jones and his teammates from South Carolina State, Mississippi Vocational lost only two games during that 1960 football season. Unfortunately, Jones's troubles off the field were not over. The authorities from Orangeburg had sent photos of him and the others to the police in Greenwood. The photos identified them as troublemakers from South Carolina. Just before Thanksgiving, the police arrived on campus and rounded up Jones and his friends. The police terrified the players, forcing them into the back of police cars to drive them out of town. The police took the players to the bus station and bought them tickets back to Florida. However,

Getting Paid to Play Football

William "Pudge" Heffelfinger became the first professional football player when, on November 13, 1892, he accepted $500, plus $25 for expenses, to play for the Allegheny Athletic Association in its game against the Pittsburgh Athletic Club. Heffelfinger scored the only points of the game.

Deacon Jones *(back row, center)* poses with South Carolina State's 1957–1958 football team. The team, known as the Bulldogs, won the state championship in 1958.

Jones decided to get off in New Orleans and spend some time with his brother, Judson.

Jones was still in New Orleans in January when the NFL held its next college draft. He did not know that Eddie Kotal, the Los Angeles Rams scout, had spoken to the Rams coach about him. Jones was amazed to learn that the Los Angeles Rams had drafted him in the fourteenth round. The dream that was supposed to be impossible had come true.

3 Deacon Jones Arrives

Today, contract negotiations between players and teams can take months and involve millions of dollars in salary and signing bonuses. Davey Jones's experience was very different. With his brother Judson, Jones waited at the airport in New Orleans to meet with Eddie Kotal, the scout who had spotted Davey tearing holes in the Florida A & M offense when he still played for South Carolina State.

Kotal walked off the plane toward the Jones brothers. Davey had already decided that whatever Kotal offered would be fine. He just wanted his signature on a professional football contract. Within minutes, he got his wish. Jones signed a contract that would pay him $7,500, plus room and board during training camp. He was so excited he did not even bother to read the

Soon after joining the Los Angeles Rams, Deacon Jones built a reputation as the premier pass-rusher of the day. Jones says his first sack came against the New York Giants' quarterback, Y.A. Tittle, at Yankee Stadium during his rookie year in 1961. "I hit him with my arms stretched out, right across his head," Jones recalled with relish in an Associated Press interview. "The blood came out." Since the term "sack" hadn't been invented yet, it was called a "smear."

contract. At that moment, the salary and terms of the one-year contract did not really matter to Jones. He only cared that he had made it to professional football.

By today's standards, a $7,500 salary seems very low. However, Jones signed his contract before the National Football League players had a union. They were not represented by agents, who help players work out their contracts. Instead, the players were at the mercy of the "generosity" of the team owners. The team owners were not anxious to cut their own profits by paying large salaries to players.

The Birth of Deacon Jones

When Deacon Jones walked onto the plane headed for training camp, he was not thinking about television contracts or money. His mind was on football.

The plane landed in Los Angeles, and Jones took a cab to his hotel. The hotel lobby was filled with reporters waiting to interview the players as they arrived. Jones was led to a microphone. Reporters shouted questions such as "Who are

Big Money

Football profits increased dramatically when television brought the sport into the homes of millions of Americans. The first football game was broadcast on October 22, 1939, by NBC. On that day, about 500 New Yorkers who were lucky enough to own TV sets watched their Brooklyn Dodgers defeat the Philadelphia Eagles 23–14. The game was shown without any commercials.

In 1960, the American Football League signed a contract with ABC to broadcast all the AFL games. ABC agreed to divide the profits earned from advertising equally among all eight teams. In 1962, the NFL signed a similar contract with CBS. In a short time, profits from these agreements were in the millions. In 1964, the NFL received $15.9 million from CBS. Today television contracts are more than $1 billion.

In the 1960s, the money earned from television contracts was paid to the team owners. As football became more popular, players began to resent the wealth that team owners earned from what the players believed was their sweat, effort, and pain on the field. In the years to come, this resentment would lead to increased conflict between the players and team owners.

you?" and "Where are you from?" Jones finally had a chance to tell the world who he was.

David Jones was such an ordinary name, he thought. He needed something that would make him stand out. He announced himself as Deacon Jones, the preacher who would bring the gospel of winning football to the people of Los Angeles and justice to the enemies of the Rams. Davey "Deacon" Jones's flashy style delighted reporters. From then on, the six-foot-five, 272-pound, fourteenth-round draft pick of the Los Angeles Rams was known as Deacon Jones.

He may have pleased the reporters, but Deacon Jones had a long way to go before he could make his mark with the Rams. On the first day of training camp, he walked onto the field to find about 100 players. Only 34 would make the team. Most of those players were white. Although football teams were not officially segregated, no team had ever carried more than six African American players. Jones would be competing to be one of those six players, not only against the newly drafted players but also against the veterans. He reacted to the competition the way he had all his life: He worked harder.

His hard work needed to pay off because Jones had discovered that, even though he had a signed contract, he could end up being cut from the team. He learned that if he did not make the team and play in the first regular season game, the Rams were not required to pay him any salary.

At first, Jones felt cheated. He felt that Eddie Kotal should have explained his contract. Jones learned a lesson that would repeat itself over and over during his career. Most team owners, including Rams owner Dan Reeves, cared about themselves first and their players later. Jones decided that the contract was not important. As long as he proved to be the best player, he would be on the field playing for the Rams when the regular season began.

Jones may have disagreed with the way Dan Reeves ran the Rams, but he could not dispute the great contributions Reeves had made to professional football. Reeves had moved the Rams to Los Angeles in 1946, making them one

Dan Reeves of the Los Angeles Rams with James D. Clark of the Philadelphia Eagles and John Mora of the New York Giants at the first meeting of the National American Football League.

of the first major league teams in any sport to play west of the Mississippi River. Over the next ten years, quarterbacks Bob Waterfield and Norm Van Brocklin had led the Los Angeles Rams offense to the divisional title in 1949, the conference title in 1955, and the NFL championship in 1951.

After 1955, however, the Rams had been less successful. In 1959 the Rams' record had fallen to 2 wins and 10 losses. Fewer fans came to Memorial Coliseum to watch the games. Owner Dan Reeves decided drastic action was necessary. He traded away nearly one-quarter of the players. He hired Bob Waterfield, the same quarterback who had led the victorious Rams a few years earlier, as head coach.

Making the Team

Deacon Jones was not concerned about Rams history when he arrived in 1961 to play his first exhibition game. In that game, the Rams beat the Washington Redskins easily, 26–7, with Jones playing both offense and defense. In all, the Rams would play five exhibition games, with

Bob Waterfield

Enshrined in the Pro Football Hall of Fame in 1965, Bob Waterfield was the National Football League's Most Valuable Player as a rookie in 1945. Waterfield led the Rams, then playing in Cleveland, to a 9–1–0 record for the season and the NFL championship. He passed for 1,609 yards and 14 touchdowns. In the title game, played on December 15, 1945, in Cleveland, the Rams defeated the Washington Redskins 15–14.

Rams star quarterback Bob Waterfield led his team, then in Cleveland, to victory in the NFL championship in his rookie year, 1945, earning himself the MVP award. The Rams, who later moved to Los Angeles, were at that time not only unbeatable, they were phenomenal in their success, once beating the Baltimore Colts 70–27. Waterfield once made a 91-yard scoring pass. He was inducted into the Hall of Fame in 1965.

the last one played in Minnesota against the Vikings. The Rams would travel directly from Minnesota to Baltimore, the site of their first regular season game. Final cuts would be made during the week between these games.

Jones's nerves were on edge. He thought how horrible it would be to have come this far, only to be sent home. The coaches announced that final cuts would be made by the Tuesday night before the Baltimore game. On Wednesday morning, Jones had still not heard whether he had made the team. He went to breakfast and found himself one of thirty-four players sitting in the cafeteria. This was the team. No fanfare. No celebration. None of the coaches made any announcement. The players finished eating and went out to practice as usual.

In his heart, Jones was celebrating. This was the team, and he was on it! Davey "Deacon" Jones, a poor, African American boy from Eatonville, Florida, had made it to the NFL!

Jones was not alone. Eleven rookies, first-year players, made the Rams squad in 1961; eight of them were African American. All

NFL Logos

The Los Angeles Rams were the first team to paint a logo on their helmets, which were then made of leather. The logo was designed in 1948 by one of the players, halfback Fred Gehrke, who had studied art in college.

The pictures above show the evolution in Rams helmet design and color.

together, counting the "taxi squad" of players carried in case of injury to the first thirty-four, the Rams had fourteen African American players. The color barrier that had kept African American athletes from playing professional sports was beginning to crumble.

Jones would face other problems. The first regular season game was against Baltimore. The Rams played well against a strong Colts team but lost 27–24. They also lost the next game, at home against the Chicago Bears. After four games, the Rams' record was 1 win and 3 losses, the last a 35–0 shutout against San Francisco.

Losing was bad enough. Even worse, the Rams seemed unable to work together. The coaches blamed the players, calling them unaggressive and sloppy. The players blamed the coaches. Bob Waterfield, the head coach, had been a great player but did not know how to unify a team, a problem that would lead to more losses.

The Losing Los Angeles Rams

4

B ob Waterfield's coaching style continued to lead the Rams to defeat. He did not push his players during practice. He expected that, as professionals, they would work their hardest. Unfortunately, this was not always true. Many of the players believed that Waterfield did not respect them, and they were not motivated to win for him. As a result, the team's performances suffered.

Waterfield had not expected to lose. He had been a great quarterback. As a rookie, he led the Rams, who were still playing in Cleveland at the time, to a divisional championship in 1945. The Rams had a winning season every year that he played, and they won NFL championships in 1945 and 1951.

Waterfield retired in 1952. There was no reason to think that he would be less successful as a coach than he had been as a player. Coaching the Rams seemed like a great opportunity. However he discovered that coaching football was very different and much more difficult for him than playing.

Waterfield coached from a distance. He let his assistants do most of the work. Most likely because he had been a quarterback, he thought the team's offense was more important than its defense. When the team won, he was quick to congratulate the offensive players. When the Rams lost, he had little to say, but he always found a way to pass the blame away from himself, usually to his defense players.

Deacon Jones found this especially annoying and unfair. Many times, he believed, the defense had kept the Rams in the game by controlling the offense of their opponents. Often the defense had played well, even though the team lost. Time and again, Jones found ways to get through to the opposing quarterback and "kill" him, tackling him behind the line of scrimmage. Jones called

Baltimore Colts quarterback Johnny Unitas *(holding ball)* is sacked by the Rams' Deacon Jones *(left)* and Lamar Lundy *(right)* in a 1961 game. Faced with the reality of meager pay, Jones came up with a creative idea to make more money at the start of his career. He talked Dan Reeves, the Rams' owner, into paying him an extra $500 for every quarterback he sacked. He made 22 sacks in 1964 and 26 in 1967.

this a "sack," total destruction of his target. He forced opposing teams to double-team him, sending two players to defend him, then figured out a way to get around them. By the end of the season, he had made 32 tackles and assisted with 16 others. He was voted the Rams Rookie of the Year—not bad for a fourteenth-round draft pick.

The Sack

Deacon Jones first used the word "sack" to describe tackling the quarterback in his own backfield. Jones said sacking a quarterback was like sacking a city—total destruction. Unofficially, based on game-day records, newspaper reports, and game films, Jones is credited with the NFL's single, regular season (1967) sack record of 26 and a career record of 180.5 (regular and postseason). The NFL did not begin recognizing the sack as a statistic until 1982, eight years after Jones retired. Jets defensive end Mark Gastineau holds the official single-season record with 22 sacks in 1984. Reggie White holds the official career record, with 137.

Deacon Jones's success earned him a new one-year contract for the 1962 season at a salary of $12,500. This seemed like a large increase. However, other rookies who were not African Americans were paid $100,000 in bonus money to sign with the Rams.

The 1962 season started as badly as the 1961 season had ended. The Rams lost their first five regular-season games. While Jones and the rest of the defense played their hearts out, Waterfield told the press that his team did not care about winning.

While the coach tried to blame his players, Dan Reeves, the Rams owner, could no longer ignore the Rams' record. He wanted to replace Waterfield, but in the middle of the season, finding a new coach would be difficult. Reeves chose Harland Svare, one of Waterfield's assistants, the defensive coach.

As a defensive lineman, Svare had been drafted by the Rams in 1953 and then traded to the Giants after the 1954 season. He became the Giants' defensive coach in 1961. During that season, the Giants' record was 10-3-1, taking

Merlin Olsen

Called the Gentle Giant, Merlin Olsen stood six-foot-five and weighed 285 pounds. He played for Utah State University and was the Rams' first-round draft pick in 1962. Lined up as defensive tackle next to Deacon Jones, Olsen completed the Fearsome Foursome, which also included Roosevelt "Rosey" Grier and Lamar Lundy. Olsen and Jones became one of the most feared defensive duos in NFL history. Using Jones's speed and Olsen's strength, they were able to outmaneuver their opponents. Coach George Allen called Olsen one of the most intelligent men ever to play the game. Olsen took advantage of any weakness or mistake made by the opposing team.

Elected to the Pro Bowl fourteen times, Olsen helped the Rams win six division titles. He played in 208 regular-season games, the last 198 in a row. He was elected to the Hall of Fame in 1982, his first year of eligibility.

After retiring from football, Olsen became a football analyst and a television star. He appeared in a regular role on the series *Little House on the Prairie*. This led to starring roles in *Father Murphy* and *Aaron's Way*.

Merlin Olsen was the perfect foil to Deacon Jones's aggressive bobbing-and-weaving style of defense. The two enjoyed a special chemistry on the field and were able to anticipate what the other had in mind. Olsen was named Rookie of the Year in 1962 and NFL Player of the Year in 1974. Olsen was also an academic achiever, being named All-American Academic and earning a master's degree in economics. He also won the Outland Trophy in 1961, awarded to the most outstanding interior lineman in college football.

them to the NFL championship game. Unfortunately, an argument with Giants head coach Allie Sherman caused Svare to leave his job after only one year. He was offered and accepted the defensive coaching job with the Rams at the start of the 1962 season.

With only five games left in an already losing season, Harland Svare replaced Bob Waterfield as head coach of the Rams. Svare believed that the team could win if they simply worked harder. When Waterfield was head coach, the Rams practiced on the field for about an hour and a half each day. Svare believed in long, hard-hitting practices, starting in the morning, with long workouts. Deacon Jones did not mind the extra practice time. More practice helped the players' skill. However, the full-contact practice games also wore them out and increased the risk of injury. Unfortunately, even with the additional practice, the Rams' record did not improve. They tied one and lost four of their last five games.

Svare responded by making the practices tougher. Even on Monday following a game, he put his players through a full-contact practice. While Bob Waterfield had let his assistants do most of the coaching, Svare was directly involved with his players. Jones had hoped that changing leadership would help the Rams. Unfortunately, although Svare's coaching methods were different, they were not more successful. Largely due to Svare's inexperience as a coach, the Rams continued to lose.

The Fearsome Foursome

Dan Reeves decided to give Svare another chance and kept him on as coach for the 1963 season. Although Deacon Jones did not know it at the time, this decision would be one of the most important for his career. Unlike quarterback Bob Waterfield, Harland Svare had played defense. His coaching centered on improving the Rams defense. Svare wanted to build his defense into the strongest in the league. He already had the beginnings: the experience of Lamar Lundy at right end, the speed of Deacon Jones at left end, and the strength of Merlin Olsen at left tackle. Svare knew exactly

The Los Angeles Rams' Fearsome Foursome: clockwise from top left: Lamar Lundy, Merlin Olsen, Deacon Jones, Roger Brown (who replaced Rosey Grier in 1967). The Fearsome Foursome changed the way football was played, inventing stunting and looping techniques, coining the term "sack," and making defense a focal point of football.

who he wanted to complete his foursome. Rosey Grier, the veteran New York Giant, had the talent and experience that Svare needed. He arranged a trade that would bring Rosey Grier to the Rams.

The creation of this defensive front four, which would become known as the Fearsome Foursome, was Svare's most important contribution to the Los Angeles Rams. Long after Svare had left as head coach, Deacon Jones and the rest of the Fearsome Foursome would terrorize other teams, working together to outmaneuver their opponents' offense with speed, strength, and surprise.

In 1963 the Rams were off to a respectable start, winning two of their first four games. Against Detroit in their fifth game, Merlin Olsen suggested that Jones hesitate for a split second after the snap, letting Olsen cross over and cut down Jones's opponent. This "stunt" opened a hole in Detroit's offensive line. Both Olsen and Jones were free to run through the hole into the backfield, throwing Detroit for a huge loss. The stunt, one of the most impressive and effective moves made by Deacon Jones and Merlin Olsen, combined Olsen's strength with Jones's speed to take their opponents by surprise.

That fall everyone in the United States experienced a huge loss. On Friday, November 22, 1963, President John F. Kennedy was assassinated in Dallas, Texas. Svare called the

President John F. Kennedy's memorial service was held at the U.S. Capitol on November 23, 1963, the day after his assassination. Kennedy's wife, Jacqueline, and daughter, Caroline, can be seen among the mourners.

team together, gave them the news, and sent them home to be with their families. None of the players or coaches believed that Sunday's game would be played.

They were wrong. The NFL owners met and decided to play the games scheduled for Sunday. The entire nation was in shock. In spite of the tragedy, while most of the nation observed a national day of mourning on Sunday, November 24, the Los Angeles Rams played the Baltimore Colts. The players, who wanted to postpone the game, were ignored.

While Deacon Jones and the Fearsome Foursome continued to play outstanding football, they were not able to carry their team to a winning season. The Rams finished the 1963 season with another disappointing record: 5 wins and 9 losses. In spite of this, Dan Reeves announced that Harland Svare was coming back for the 1964 season. In fact, Svare would continue as coach through the 1965 season, posting losing records of 5 wins, 7 losses, and 2 ties in 1964 and 4 wins and 10 losses in 1965.

Finally, Dan Reeves could not ignore the anger of the Rams fans or the ridicule of newspaper reporters. He found a new coach, George Allen, who had been the defensive coach of the Chicago Bears. Under George Allen, the fortunes of the Rams would finally turn and Deacon Jones would become one of the best defensive players the NFL had ever seen.

Deacon Jones and the Winning Rams

As a coach, George Allen was everything that Harland Svare was not. Svare blamed his players and punished them for losing by running bone-crushing, full-contact practices every day. Allen inspired his players with encouragement and praise. His practices were hard, but they were not designed simply to inflict pain. Allen drilled his players so that their skills would improve. He demanded that they be in top physical shape. He told them over and over again that deep down, the Rams were winners; they needed to believe in themselves. If they worked together and played their hardest, the Rams would be unstoppable.

Allen was exactly the kind of coach Deacon Jones needed. Jones had always worked as hard

Jubilant Rams players and officials carry head coach George Allen off the field after a victory over the Green Bay Packers in 1967. Though the Rams lost to the Packers at the Super Bowl, 1967 heralded the winning times ahead, with Deacon Jones personally making 26 of the team's 43 sacks that season. Jones was also named Most Valuable Defensive Player of the Year.

"You must reach beyond your abilities, recognize that no talent, without hard work, can make you a winner. You must be honest with yourself—and with others. There is no easy way to success."

—George Allen

as he could. With Svare as coach, though, Jones had been working for his own pride only. He had been playing for a team that did not believe it could win. Allen asked for and listened to suggestions from his players. They responded by practicing harder. They could see that the drills paid off; they were getting better.

The 1966 Season

Even though the Rams won three of their five preseason exhibition games, the press wrote them off, expecting another year of losing. The Rams opened the regular season with a history-making game against the Atlanta Falcons. The Falcons were playing their first game ever and were determined to enter the record books with a victory. After a gritty, hard-fought battle, however, it was the Rams who wrote history, winning the game 19–14.

During the second game in Chicago, the Bears took a 17–14 lead into the locker room at half time. Jones and the Fearsome Foursome, however, held the Bears scoreless in the second half. The Rams won again. The next week, the Rams faced the mighty Green Bay Packers. Jones played inspired football. He slammed his arm against the helmet of his opponents. Jones became famous for this move, called a headslap. It would eventually be outlawed because the risk of injury to Jones's victims was so great. During the game, the Rams defense forced six fumbles and hounded Packers quarterback Bart Starr. Fearing for their running game, the Packers switched to a passing attack and took a 24–13 victory.

Despite the loss, the Rams had proven two things. First, they would fight to the end and would never give another team an easy victory. Second, the Foursome was truly fearsome.

George Allen *(standing, third from left)* pumps up the Rams defensive team during the third quarter of a game against the Washington Redskins in 1967.

George Allen inspired Deacon Jones. He told the young man that he would be a legend someday. Allen knew the Rams were winners and that their spirit had not been destroyed.

Although the Rams offense struggled to keep up with the defense, the Rams ended the 1966 season with an 8-6 record, their first winning season in more than ten years.

1967: Another Winning Season

The 1967 season, Deacon Jones's seventh year in the NFL, began in glory. The Rams opened with their first unbeaten preseason ever. Their defense seemed to get stronger and stronger. Deacon Jones was the center of that strength.

Every team the Rams faced was forced to come up with a special strategy to try and stop Jones. They would double- and triple-team him, sending two or three players at him at once. Of course, sending so many players after him left openings in other parts of the opposing offense. The rest of the Fearsome Foursome took over, taking advantage of these weaknesses to stun opponents.

During the week between games, Jones loved to remind his upcoming opponents what to expect. His job was to "kill" quarterbacks, and he intended to do just that. He let his ferocious attitude speak for him during interviews between games. His performance on the field during games spoke even louder.

George Allen continued to motivate his players, treating them like the winners he knew them to be. He held a meeting each Thursday to celebrate the upcoming victory on Sunday. The following Tuesday, he held an awards ceremony to recognize the outstanding individual play of his team.

The results during the 1967 season, a 9-1-2 record, showed just how outstanding that play

"You hadn't lived until you had your bell rung by Deacon a few times."

—Ron Mix, offensive tackle, San Diego Chargers/Oakland Raiders, 1979 Hall of Fame enshrinee was. The season was not over, however. The Rams were looking for a championship. They would have to beat the Packers and the Colts to get there.

At first, it looked like the Rams would not make it. With less than a minute left in the game against Green Bay, the Packers had a 24–20 lead. A good, deep punt and four plays were all the Packers needed to kill the Rams' championship dreams. But the Rams were not going away. Their never-say-die attitude paid off, as Jones and the special team's defense broke through the Packers' line and blocked the punt. The Rams scored to take the lead and the game.

Despite their loss to the Rams, the Packers had already won the Central Division Championship. To win the Coastal Division and move on to Super Bowl II, the Rams still had to beat the Colts.

The Rams led Baltimore 10–7 in the second quarter, but the Colts had the ball deep in Rams territory. One completed pass from Colts quarterback Johnny Unitas would put the ball in the end zone and give the Colts the lead. Instead, as Unitas dropped back to pass, Jones

MEETING

MONDAY 11^{30}

GET THE COLTS.

George Allen looks over his shoulder at a blackboard in the Rams dressing room. Having just beaten the Green Bay Packers, their next game was against the Baltimore Colts. The Rams' strategy was simple, "Get the Colts."

hit him and knocked him off balance. Unitas let the ball fly, but it was intercepted by the Rams. The turnover led to a Rams touchdown and the greatest victory in Rams history. The Rams were the Coastal Division champs.

Once again, the Green Bay Packers stood between the Rams and their championship goal. This time, though, the Rams would not be victorious. The game was played in Wisconsin on an icy field in frigid temperatures. The Packers easily defeated the Rams, 28–7. Despite the loss, the Rams finished the season with the best win-loss record in the team's history.

As a result of his outstanding play that season, Deacon Jones finished second to Johnny Unitas in the voting for Most Valuable Player in the NFL. Jones was named Most Valuable Defensive Player. During the season, he had made a record 100 unassisted tackles and 26 sacks. A few weeks later, on January 27, 1968, the towns of Orlando and Eatonville, Florida, held a parade to celebrate "Deacon Jones Day."

Football and Politics

6

Before the next season began, Deacon Jones took an unexpected turn back to politics. As a young man, he faced discouraging experiences in the civil rights movement that had convinced him to stick to football. The assassinations of John F. Kennedy and Martin Luther King Jr. had only driven him farther away.

It was a conversation with his old friend and Fearsome Foursome partner Rosey Grier that changed Jones's mind. Grier asked Jones to help provide security for Robert Kennedy, JFK's younger brother, on his presidential campaign trail. After some discussion, Jones agreed. He spent the next few months traveling with Kennedy, guiding him through the crowds. Jones swore that what had happened to Martin Luther King would not happen to Robert Kennedy.

Senator Robert Kennedy talks to his security detail, Deacon Jones *(right)*, Rosey Grier *(far left)*, and a player from the Chicago Bears, while touring Indianapolis for the primaries on May 4, 1968.

Sadly, Jones was wrong. While celebrating his victory in the California Democratic primary, Kennedy was gunned down by Sirhan Sirhan. Jones had a speaking engagement in Denver and was not with Kennedy that night. The feeling that he could have perhaps prevented Kennedy's death would haunt Deacon Jones forever.

Strike

A different kind of politics affected Jones's life as the 1968 football season began. Over 600

The Assassination of Robert Kennedy

On June 5, 1968, Sirhan Sirhan moved through the crowd of people surrounding Robert Kennedy. As he got closer to Kennedy, Sirhan began shooting, firing eight shots. Rosey Grier and Olympic hero Rafer Johnson, hired to protect Kennedy, grabbed Sirhan and held him until the police arrived. Tragically, like his brother, President John F. Kennedy, Robert Kennedy died from his gunshot wounds.

Rosey Grier helps to subdue Sirhan Sirhan after the assassin shot Robert Kennedy on June 5, 1968.

players went on strike, refusing to report for spring training. The conflict centered around money. While the amount of money paid by television stations to the team owners had skyrocketed, pro football players didn't reap any of the benefits. The players were locked into contracts, signed years earlier, which kept their salaries low. They wanted a bigger share of the profits, and they believed that they deserved it. They argued that they were responsible for playing the game that fans came out to see and advertisers paid to sponsor. Without them, stadium seats would be empty.

The team owners, however, had all the power. Players did not yet have agents and could not choose their own teams as free agents, as they can today. The owners decided when, where, and if the players would play. In the summer of 1968, the owners voted to lock the striking players out of training camp.

For Deacon Jones, there were bigger issues than salary and benefits at stake. He believed that players should have more control over their careers. He also wanted to discuss openly the differences in salary between white and African American players. Jones tried to convince other players that the NFL should join a union, like the Teamsters. The union would represent the players and negotiate for higher salaries and pension benefits. Because so many people in many different kinds of jobs belonged to the Teamsters, the organization was very powerful. Jones believed this power would help football players get more control over their careers.

Most players, though, were more concerned with increasing their own salaries. They did not think about long-term results. They turned down Jones's suggestion of joining a union, and instead let a few players deal with the owners. These players accepted an offer that increased their pension benefits but did not affect the larger issues that Jones believed were so important.

The strike was officially settled in July, and most players returned to training camp. Jones and a few other players, including Merlin Olsen and Rosey Grier, believed that the players had given in too soon. They still refused to play. The Rams owners, however, were unmoved. Olsen suggested that they negotiate together, but Jones refused. Later, looking back at the strike, Jones would admit that this decision had been a mistake. Because they acted individually, each player was powerless against the owners' united determination not to give in to the players' demands. Olsen was the first to return to camp. Grier retired from pro football.

It made no difference that Jones was now a superstar in the NFL. His choices were to sit out his contract with the Rams for the next two years and hope that another team would want him in 1970, or to rejoin the team. He chose to play. He returned to the Rams without any changes in the contract he had signed two years before.

1968: More Wins for the Rams

The Rams began their 1968 season with victories. The St. Louis Cardinals, Pittsburgh Steelers, Cleveland Browns, San Francisco 49ers, Green Bay Packers, and Atlanta Falcons fell as the Rams defense led its team to a 6–0 record. Their rampage was stopped briefly by the Baltimore Colts. But the Rams were a team with a mission;

Rosey Grier began his career with the New York Giants before forming the fourth pillar in the Rams' Fearsome Foursome defense. His teammates said that Grier was incapable of anger and was so gentle that he tried to tackle the offense in a way that wouldn't hurt them. Though he was effective, this may have cost him a place in the Hall of Fame. Here he is seen engrossed in one of his hobbies, needlepoint, making a tennis racket cover.

nothing would keep them from the NFL championship game. Jones did not let injury or illness keep him from playing. Even with the flu, he struggled out of bed to lead the Rams to a 31–3 victory over the Vikings. With two games left in the regular season, the Rams' record was 10-1-1. Only the Chicago Bears and Baltimore Colts stood between the Rams and their goal.

Unfortunately, it was not only the talents of the Chicago Bears that would work against the Rams. Toward the end of the game, the officials miscalled second down when the Rams actually had first down. Naturally, this altered the Rams offense, forcing a long "Hail Mary" pass that was risky. The pass fell incomplete. Two plays later, the Bears took over with five seconds left in the game. The Rams' chance at victory had been stolen by NFL officials.

The officiating crew was suspended, but that did not change the result of the game. The Rams had lost and were robbed of their chance at the championship. The Baltimore Colts beat the dejected Rams the following week in a game that no longer mattered. Even Jones's election to the Pro Bowl that year did not make up for the lost championship. George Allen fully believed the Rams should be in the Super Bowl and said so to the press, angering owner Dan Reeves.

Rescuing George Allen

George Allen's winning record should have protected him from Dan Reeves's personal feelings. Reeves resented Allen. He knew the players had great respect for their coach. While other owners might have seen this as a benefit, Reeves saw it as a threat. He wanted control over his team. On Christmas Day 1968, he called Allen and fired him.

What Is the Pro Bowl?

The season-ending Pro Bowl pits the all-stars of the American Football Conference and the National Football Conference against each other. Coaches, players, and fans vote to choose the forty-three-man rosters. Each group's vote counts as one-third. No other sport combines voting by fans, coaches, and players to choose its all-star teams.

In the first Pro Bowl, played on January 14, 1951, the American Conference All-Stars defeated the National Conference All-Stars, 28–27 at Memorial Coliseum in Los Angeles. Since 1980 the Pro Bowl has been played in Honolulu, Hawaii. In 2001, the Pro Bowl celebrated its fiftieth anniversary.

Lamar Lundy defends fired head coach George Allen (in dark glasses) along with other Rams' players Deacon Jones *(left)*, Charlie Cowan, and Merlin Olsen *(right)*. Their protest helped get Allen reinstated to his position.

Reeves did not realize how deep the team's loyalty to George Allen went. Deacon Jones gathered the Rams players and organized them to force Dan Reeves to rehire George Allen. Eight players, including Jones, Lamar Lundy, and quarterback Roman Gabriel, signed a pledge of loyalty announcing they would quit unless Allen came back. The players set up a picket line around the Rams office. Ticket sales were down, as fans, who had thrilled to the Rams' recent success, supported the players.

As the days went by, both sides fought their battle in the press. The Rams management accused Allen of tricking other teams out of their draft choices. These rumors were never proven. The facts did prove George Allen's winning record. Pressure from players and fans finally proved too strong. On January 7, 1969, George Allen returned as head coach of the Rams.

Deacon Jones's strength, instrumental in George Allen's return to the Rams, had held against the team owners just as it held against his opponents in the field. He considered his part in keeping Allen with the Rams to be one of his most important accomplishments.

1969–1970: The Last Allen Years

George Allen's contract kept him with the Rams for two more years. In 1969 the Rams earned a place in the Western Conference championship game, only to lose to the Minnesota Vikings. Under the coaching of George Allen, Deacon Jones and the Rams had become the winners Allen always knew they were. The fans were in love with Deacon Jones's hard-hitting, head-slapping style.

> "Every man is free to rise as far as he is able or willing, but it is only the degree to which he thinks or believes that determines the degree to which he will rise."
>
> —Deacon Jones

A fan held a sign during home games that named Jones the "Secretary of Defense." The press picked up the nickname and it stuck.

The Rams began their 1970 season by winning all of their preseason games. From the beginning of the season, rumors spread that George Allen would leave when the season was over. The more successful the Rams were on the field, the louder the rumors rang. Allen tried to shut them down. He knew the rumors were bad for team spirit. He wanted his players to concentrate on what was happening this season, not what might happen next season.

The Rams were in first place and were once more on their way to another chance at the championship. George Allen's contract would expire December 31, but Dan Reeves had not

In 1967, Jones was voted NFL Defensive Player of the Year. Jones set five NFL records that year, marking the best season ever for a defensive player. Here, Jones goes through the rope drill at the Rams' practice field in Los Angeles.

made a decision. Deacon Jones wondered who would coach the Rams the next year. The logical choice seemed to be George Allen, the winningest coach in Rams history. However, it soon became clear the logic would not play a part in Dan Reeves's decision. Finally, on the last day of his contract, Reeves called Allen to say he would not be rehired. Three days later, Dan Reeves announced that Tommy Prothro, a successful college coach with no professional experience, would replace George Allen.

Allen's success, of course, had not gone unnoticed. He became the head coach of the Washington Redskins. The Rams were happy to trade several of their players to the Redskins, but Deacon Jones was not one of them. Jones wanted desperately to go with Allen, but the Rams management would not agree to a trade.

The first year that Tommy Prothro coached, the Rams finished in second place, largely based on the strength of George Allen's program. After that, Prothro would never again coach his team to a winning season. In contrast, throughout his twelve years as head coach in the pros, George Allen never had a losing season.

Deacon Jones's Final Years on the Field

Dan Reeves, who had been suffering from cancer, died soon after hiring Tommy Prothro as head coach of the Los Angeles Rams. The 1971 Rams season, then, began with a new coach and a new owner. However, the new combination would not be able to continue the winning record.

In his eager attempt to separate himself from George Allen, Prothro quickly destroyed the team's discipline and winning spirit. He shortened practices and announced that everyone, including veterans, would need to earn their spots on the team. Where in the past the Rams had won largely due to their outstanding defense, Prothro announced that his focus would be on the offense. In addition, because many Rams veterans had been traded to George Allen's Redskins, Prothro was often forced to use less-experienced players.

Even before the season started, Deacon Jones knew that Prothro's lack of experience in coaching professional football would be a problem. Jones could not help but compare Prothro to former coach George Allen. The most glaring difference proved to be the way each coach treated the players. Allen had encouraged and praised his players, instilling a winning team spirit. Prothro, on the other hand, blamed the players for the team's losses,

The Unlucky Rams

In 1979 the Los Angeles Rams won the NFC Championship for the first time and made it to Super Bowl XIV. They were defeated by the Pittsburgh Steelers 31–19. On January 30, 2000, after moving to St. Louis, the Rams would finally become Super Bowl champions, defeating the Tennessee Titans 23–16 to win Super Bowl XXXIV.

even when it was clear that coaching errors had caused the defeats.

Many players, including Deacon Jones, still played with George Allen's coaching in mind. Near the end of the season, the Rams had a 7-4-1 record, a respectable start for a new coach. The Rams were still in contention for the divisional championship. They needed to win their next game to secure it. Ironically, that game was against George Allen's Washington Redskins.

Allen got his revenge, defeating the Rams 38–24 and knocking them out of the play-offs. That game was also the beginning of the end of Tommy Prothro's career with the Rams. Although he would return in 1972 for one more season, the Rams would suffer their first losing season since the arrival of George Allen, with a disappointing 6-7-1 record.

An Unexpected Turn

Another big loss most likely contributed to the 1972 losing record of the Rams. Deacon Jones was not part of the team. In January, while he

After his time with the Rams, Jones played two years with the San Diego Chargers and one with the Washington Redskins, but was never able to win the elusive Super Bowl ring.

was attending Roman Gabriel's wedding, Jones received a call from Tommy Prothro. Jones had been traded to the San Diego Chargers, who were, ironically, coached by Harland Svare, the old Rams coach. Jones's trade was justified as part of the Rams "youth movement." The Rams received future draft choices for younger players in exchange for Deacon Jones, the experienced Secretary of Defense.

When Jones learned about the trade, he considered refusing it. Instead of playing for the Chargers, he could walk away from football at the height of his career. Harland Svare, however, convinced Jones that he would work as a player-coach. Hopefully, this would lead to a coaching job once Jones decided to stop playing. Svare had great respect for Jones and understood that his experience would make him an excellent coach. Encouraged, Jones decided to make the move.

The first regular game of the season pitted the Chargers against the Rams. Although the Rams had traded their aging defensive end in favor of youth, they were still forced to

double-team Deacon Jones on every play. The
Rams spent so much energy trying to stop
Jones that the Chargers were able to break
down the Rams offensive line and stop them.
The Chargers won 14–13.

"Old" Deacon Jones had beaten the youth
movement of the Rams. However, the rest of the
Chargers' season would not go as well. At the
end of 1972, Jones again found himself on a
losing team coached by Harland Svare, as the
Chargers ended with a 4-9-1 record.

Jones had never expected the Chargers to
win with Svare as their coach. He believed that
Svare would have a short Charger career. Soon
the owners would start looking for a new coach.
Jones hoped to be the man they chose.

At the end of the 1972 season, Gene Klein,
the owner of the Chargers, offered Jones an
assistant coaching job when he decided to stop
playing. At first, Jones was excited at the
prospect. This could be the chance he needed to
step up to a head coach position. However, he
was worried that he would never have that
opportunity. He was sure that he did not want

to end his career as an assistant coach. Jones asked Klein if he believed such an opportunity would be a possibility in the future. Klein flatly said "no." At that time, no professional football team had an African American coach or would consider hiring one. Jones was angry and refused the assistant coaching job.

Deacon Jones stayed one more year with the Chargers. During that 1973 season, a drug scandal exposed the fact that players relied on painkillers provided by their teams to survive the physical punishment that football required. Largely because he was a celebrity, Jones had been singled out and was fined $3,000. He denied drug abuse charges and refused to pay the fine.

Football was no longer fun for Deacon Jones. His heart was not in the game. Years of physical punishment had taken their toll. The thrill of "killing" quarterbacks was gone. Then Jones heard from George Allen. If Jones wanted it, there was a spot for him on the Washington Redskins. Jones would not be the heart of the defense, but he would end his career playing for George Allen.

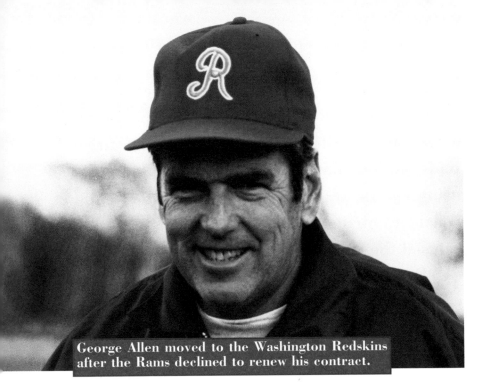

George Allen moved to the Washington Redskins after the Rams declined to renew his contract.

In spite of all his success, Jones still had one more football dream. Before he retired, he wanted to play in the Super Bowl. Jones knew that the Redskins would have a chance at the Super Bowl because George Allen's teams were winners. As a Redskin, Jones did not start in most games. Instead, Jones specialized in rushing the quarterback whenever he was forced to pass for long yardage on third down.

With two games left in the season, the Redskins faced the Rams. No one wanted to win that game more than Deacon Jones. George Allen knew it and decided to start Jones. His decision proved to be the right one. The Redskins won 23–17, one of the most satisfying victories of Jones's career.

The Redskins faced the Chicago Bears in the last regular season game of Deacon Jones's career. The Redskins took no prisoners as they destroyed the Bears 41–0. Remarkably, Jones, who had always practiced as a backup kicker, kicked the extra point after the final touchdown. It was the first and only time Deacon Jones kicked during a game.

The Redskins faced the Rams again in the NFL divisional play-off. This time, it was the Rams who got revenge, beating the Redskins 19–10. Deacon Jones would end his career without a trip to the Super Bowl.

Jones would, however, earn a trip to Canton, Ohio. In 1980, five years after he retired from the game, and the first year he was eligible, Deacon Jones was enshrined forever in the Football Hall of Fame.

The Hall of Fame

Because George Allen had played such an important role in Deacon Jones's career, Jones asked Allen to introduce him to the players and guests who attended the induction ceremony at the Hall of Fame. Allen was honored. In his introduction, Allen described Jones as a natural

The Pro Football Hall of Fame

Canton, Ohio, was chosen as the site of the Pro Football Hall of Fame on April 27, 1961. The choice was significant because Canton was where the professional football league, which would later become the NFL, was born in 1920. Two years later, in 1963, the Hall of Fame opened its doors to visitors and enshrined seventeen charter members: Sammy Baugh, Bert Bell, Joe Carr, Earl "Dutch" Clark, Red Grange, George Halas, Mel Hein, Wilbur "Pete" Henry, Cal Hubbard, Don Hutson, Earl "Curly" Lambeau, Tim Mara, George Preston Marshall, Johnny "Blood" McNally, Bronko Nagurski, Ernie Nevers, and Jim Thorpe.

leader who helped Allen maintain team discipline. "By his pure energy of action," Allen said, "Deacon was the inspirational leader on every team on which he played." Allen was glad to have the opportunity to share his thoughts on Jones's accomplishments. "A Secretary of Defense, Deacon was the most feared defensive player in the league," Allen told the crowd. "The opposition often built their entire offensive game plan around him. No one man could block him." That year, 1980, was an election year. "Regardless of who wins the presidency this fall," said Allen, "the first Cabinet appointee should be Deacon Jones as Secretary of Defense."

In his speech that day, Deacon Jones reminisced about his struggle to achieve recognition and success in life and on the football field. "Early in life," he said, "I learned that all life is a purpose for struggle." The most important choice we make in life, according to Jones, is choosing our life's goal. Once the goal is understood, we need help to achieve it. Jones attributed his success to the

FOOTBALL HALL OF FAME

Deacon Jones *(second from right)* at his Hall of Fame induction ceremony in 1980, holding a bust of himself, which would be placed inside.

support and love of his family, and to George Allen. "It has been said that the man who produces an idea in any field of endeavor, the man who discovers new knowledge is the permanent benefactor of humanity," Jones said. "The man who discovers my knowledge and ability, who challenges it and finds it and without whose guidance I would not be here today is George Allen."

Jones thanked all the players with whom he played, both in college and professionally. He shared with everyone the five points that make a champion: teamwork, hard work, pride, determination, and competitive spirit. All champions share "the feeling of excitement in solving problems, the delight of taking on a new challenge, and the eagerness to meet another hard challenge," he said.

As he was enshrined in the Pro Football Hall of Fame, Deacon Jones's quest for championship became a reality.

Life After Football

8

Deacon Jones was and is a celebrity. While he was still playing pro football, he found time for guest appearances on television shows like, *The Brady Bunch*, *Bewitched*, *The Odd Couple*, and *The Merv Griffin Show*. For a while, he thought about a career in music.

After his extraordinary football career ended, Deacon Jones continued to earn honors. He was named the Most Valuable Ram of All Time by the *Los Angeles Times* and the Defensive End of the Century by *Sports Illustrated*.

Jones loves to talk about football, combining his knowledge with wit and humor. He has appeared on many football television shows, including *Up Close*, *Hardcore Football*, *Monday Night Live*, and *Pro Magazine*. He has entertained fans in the Rams' broadcast booth. Just as he always has, as part of the team on Fox Sports Network's *NFL This Morning*, he "tells it like it is." He has also written a column for *TuffStuff* magazine.

Jones's popularity and sense of style have made him a natural spokesman for corporations. He has worked for Haggar Slacks, the Miller Brewing Company, Epson America, and Pacific Coast Medical Enterprises.

Deacon Jones understands that those who have been more fortunate in life should work to help those who have less. In 1997 he founded the Deacon Jones Foundation. By providing college scholarships and mentoring programs, the organization gives inner-city youth the tools they need to escape poverty and violence.

Because he was diagnosed with high-blood pressure when he left the Rams, Jones works to increase public awareness about this condition, reminding people to check their blood pressure regularly. He also encourages a healthy, low-fat diet and exercise.

Deacon Jones's Statistics

- NFL All-Pro 10 times
- Pro Bowl nine times
- NFL Most Valuable Defensive Player 1967 and 1968
- NFL Hall of Fame
- South Carolina Hall of Fame
- Florida Hall of Fame
- South Carolina State College Hall of Fame
- Record: Single-season sack leader in the 1967 regular season with 26 (with postseason 32)
- Record: Unofficial career sack leader with 180 (official sack statistics were not kept until 1982)
- Record: Career solo tackles—downed 752 linemen

Perhaps the most important contribution that Deacon Jones has made to professional football is his drive to always be the best. Through his example, young football players on any level can learn to work hard and practice hard, for themselves and for their teams.

Timeline

1920   The first professional football league forms as the American Professional Football Association.

1921   The American Professional Football Association is renamed the National Football League.

1938   David "Deacon" Jones is born.

1939   On October 22, NBC televises the first professional football game. The Philadelphia Eagles beat the Brooklyn Dodgers, 23–14.

1946   The All-American Football Conference begins.

1946   Post-World War II football integrates when the Cleveland Browns sign Marion Motley and Bill Willis, and the Los Angeles Rams sign Woody Strode and Kenny Washington.

1946   The Cleveland Rams move to Los Angeles, becoming the Los Angeles Rams.

1947   Jackie Robinson begins playing first base for the Brooklyn Dodgers.

1950   The National Football League and the All-American Football Conference merge.

1954 In *Brown v. the Board of Education*, the United States Supreme Court rules against school segregation.

1957 Deacon Jones arrives at South Carolina State College.

1960 The American Football League is born.

1961 Deacon Jones is drafted in the fourteenth round of the college football draft by the Los Angeles Rams.

1963 President John F. Kennedy is assassinated.

1963 National Football Hall of Fame opens to the public.

1966 George Allen takes over as coach of the Rams. The Rams have their first winning season since 1958.

1967 Deacon Jones is chosen the NFL's Most Valuable Defensive Player for the first time.

1968 Deacon Jones is chosen the NFL's Most Valuable Defensive Player for the second time.

1970 ABC launches the first season of *Monday Night Football*.

1970 The National Football Conference (NFC) and the American Football Conference (AFC) are formed.

1980 Deacon Jones is inducted into the National Football Hall of Fame.

Glossary

backfield Area of the football field behind the linemen.

boycott Making the choice to stop buying or using something in order to protest the way it is made, sold, or used, or the way its manufacturer conducts business.

civil disobedience Disobeying laws believed to be unjust, without the use of violence.

integration Bringing together people of different races, ages, genders, or cultural backgrounds.

intercept Gaining possession of an opponent's pass.

line of scrimmage Yard line on a football field where the play will begin.

lineman Player on offense or defense who begins the play on the line of scrimmage.

prejudice Making a negative judgment about strangers based on their skin color, ethnicity, gender, religion, size, or income level.

racial discrimination Giving one race of people preference over another.

racial segregation Separating one group of people from another based on their race.

sack To tackle a quarterback behind the line of scrimmage.

sit-in Form of civil disobedience where a group of protestors sits down to block access to a place.

snap Pass that initiates each play; hike.

turnover Loss of possession of the ball.

For More Information

Deacon Jones Foundation
446 S. Anaheim Hills Road, Suite 186
Anaheim Hills, CA 92807

National Football League
280 Park Avenue
New York, NY 10017
Web site: http://www.nfl.com

Professional Football Hall of Fame
212 George Halas Drive NW
Canton, OH 44708
(330) 456-8207
Web site: http://www.profootballhof.com

Professional Football Researchers Association
12870 Route 30
N. Huntingdon, PA 15642
Web site: http://www.footballresearch.com

Web Sites

Due to the changing nature of Internet links, the Rosen Publishing Group, Inc., has developed an online list of Web sites related to the subject of this book. This site is updated regularly. Please use this link to access the list:

http://www.rosenlinks.com/fhf/djon/

For Further Reading

Klawitter, John, ed. *The Book of Deacon: The Wit and Wisdom of Deacon Jones*. Santa Ana, CA: Seven Lock Press, 2001.

Klawitter, John, and Deacon Jones. *Headslap: The Life and Times of Deacon Jones*. New York: Prometheus Books,1996.

McDonough, William, et al. *The NFL Century: The Complete Story of the National Football League, 1920–2000*. New York: Smithmark Publishers, 1999.

National Football League. *NFL's Greatest: Pro Football's Best Players, Teams and Games*. New York: NFL Publishing, 2001.

National Football League. *NFL 2001 Record and Fact Book*. New York: NFL Publishing, 2001.

Bibliography

Aiken, Miles, and Peter Rowe. *American Football: The Records*. Enfield, England: Guinness Books, 1986.

Cyber Nation Web Site. Retrieved October 2001 (http://www.cyber-nation.com).

Hill, Gary. "Jackie Robinson Was Never Satisfied." Retrieved September 2001 (http://www.sound.net).

Jarrett, William S. *Timetables of Sports History: Football*. New York: Facts on File, 1989.

Klawitter, John, ed. *The Book of Deacon: The Wit and Wisdom of Deacon Jones*. Santa Ana, CA: Seven Lock Press, 2001.

Klawitter, John, and Deacon Jones. *Headslap: The Life and Times of Deacon Jones*. New York: Prometheus Books, 1996.

McDonough, William, et al. *The NFL Century: The Complete Story of the National Football League, 1920–2000*. New York: Smithmark Publishers 1999.

National Football League. *NFL's Greatest: Pro Football's Best Players, Teams and Games*. New York: NFL Publishing, 2001.

National Football League. *NFL 2001 Record and Fact Book*. New York: NFL Publishing, 2001.

National Football League Web Site. Retrieved October 2001 (http://www.nfl.com).

NPR. Elson, John, "And Now, Who Shot R.F.K.?" National Public Radio, June 7, 1993. Retrieved September 2001 (http://homepages.tcp.co.uk/~dlewis/timerev.htm).

Professional Football Researchers Association. Gershman, Michael. "Merlin Olsen: Gentlemanly Giant." Retrieved September 2001 (http://www.footballresearch.com).

Sporting News Web Site. Retrieved September–October 2001 (http://www.sportingnews.com).

Index

About the Author

Karen Donnelly is a freelance writer living in Connecticut with her husband, David, and her daughters, Cathy and Colleen. She has written several books for the Rosen Publishing Group, including *Coping with Dyslexia* and *Leprosy*.

Photo Credits

Cover © Sporting News/Icon; pp. 4, 7, 38, 42 (top left and right), 46–47, 54, 59, 62–63, 67, 70, 71, 78, 90 © Bettmann/Corbis; p. 10 © Corbis; pp. 13, 16, 33, 40, 42 (bottom right), 81, 94–95 © AP/Wide World Photos; pp. 19, 28 © Hulton/Archive/Getty Images; pp. 24, 31 © South Carolina State University; pp. 42 (bottom left), 56 © Wally McNamee/Corbis; pp. 51, 86 © Sports Chrome; p. 75 © Michael Rougier/Timepix.

Series Design and Layout

Tahara Hasan